For a Life Worth Living

A Workbook for Actively and Purposefully Living Your Life

Karen Mills-Alston

This edition is published by
That Guy's House in 2020

ISBN: 978-1913479-09-1

www.ThatGuysHouse.com

That Guy's House

Also by Karen Mills-Alston

10 Principles for A Life Worth Living—A Guide for Actively and Purposefully Living Your Life.

10 Principles for A Life Worth Living—Practicing Spiritual Principles Daily Through the Use of Affirmations.

Introduction

PRACTICE, PRACTICE, PRACTICE

That which transforms your life is what you practice. And what you practice constitutes your personal laws of life—not what you merely believe in, but what you practice. It's all well and good to read books and to attend seminars, lectures and workshops and to say, "Oh, that really resonates with me! It's now part of my life's philosophy." Your philosophy may give you a temporary state of euphoria, but if your want to be anchored in Reality, it takes practice, practice, practice. We are not here to be euphoric but to get free. Rudimentary spirituality is theory; advanced spirituality is practice. What you practice, you ultimately embody, paving the way for breakthroughs, insight, fresh realizations and the evolutions of consciousness. In truth, that which is inconceivable is caught and understood by those who are making their spiritual practices a way of life.

Michael Bernard Beckwith
Spiritual Liberation

WELCOME TO YOUR UNIQUE YOU!

Welcome to this new moment of your Beingness where there is life, joy, abundance, beauty, and so much more. You may not even know this yet, but it's true! Take a breath. Let go, surrender, and yield to the Universal Presence that loves you more than you can possibly imagine. It birthed Itself as you at this particular time to recall your gifts, talents, and capabilities to be developed and given generously to this planet. Begin to open your heart now. Only you can do the work necessary for your own expansion. NO ONE can do it for you, nor can you do it for anyone else. As they say—"It's an inside job." Know this—you are needed and necessary! There is ALWAYS an opportunity to begin again, letting go of your "little self" and activating the idea that life is for living fully NOW. It's time to free yourself from limiting habits, patterns, and false beliefs that stop you from being your REAL self! How sweet and wonderful it is to release your smallness and allow that which you came here to BE to emerge! Michael Bernard Beckwith has said, "Let me have the strength to be the REAL me!" That's the importance of this workbook—to practice getting out of your smallness and setting in motion your potentiality, standing strong in your uniqueness AS YOU! No one can stop you! If you are willing to do the work necessary, even when it's hard and painful, this workbook is for you. Let your Soul say YES! Welcome home!

Blessings and so much love!
Karen Mills-Alston, ALSP

How to Use This Book

I am grateful you have selected this workbook. You may or may not be familiar with Agape's Seven Spiritual Practices—affirmative prayer, meditation, Life Visioning, sacred service, spiritual fellowship, spiritual study, and tithing. These "..... Seven Spiritual Practices form the matrix of individual spiritual evolution. While there are many adjunct practices that assist in the expansion of consciousness, it is these seven that have proved themselves to accelerate spiritual awakening of practitioners of the world's wisdom traditions." There is a Universal Law and Power back of these practices. This workbook is based on some of these Spiritual Practices. We get to choose to use these Spiritual Practices **consistently** as we create a life that we are meant to live! Remember, Universal Law is impersonal. It is "neutral, unbiased, nonpartisan, unprejudiced, objective, detached, disinterested, dispassionate, without favoritism." I am reminded that "*As A Man Thinketh* is an essay and self-help classic, which argues that the key to mastering your life is harnessing the power of your thoughts and helps you cultivate the philosophy and attitude of a positive, successful person." What this truly means is that our life is a reflection of where we have placed our thoughts, where we have placed our attention. As human beings, it's easy to walk in lock step with the world and linger in worry, doubt, and fear. As Divine Beings, we get to remember we have everything we need within us that is simply waiting to be activated, to be remembered. AND THAT TAKES PRACTICE!

When I was a kid living in my metaphysical consciousness, I often made lists of intentions. There were things I wanted to get, do, or have in my life. Each time an intention was demonstrated, I thought, "This really works! What if I did this all the time?" What I know now is that even at an early age, I was tapping into the Infinite Possibilities of living a magnificent life. I never had a consistent, intentional Spiritual Practice until I matured and began my studies at Agape International Spiritual Center, founded and directed by Michael Bernard Beckwith. My Spiritual Practice includes affirmative prayer, meditation, Life Visioning, sacred service, spiritual fellowship, spiritual study, tithing. This workbook encourages you to incorporate some or all of these Spiritual Practices into your life.

I had a client who came to me in a very low, emotional place. He was frustrated, angry, sad, and had no idea his next step. I asked a simple question—"Are you meditating?" His response—"Sometimes." I have learned the importance of having a consistent Spiritual Practice. Practicing "sometimes" allows your life to be "sometimey." What this means is that your life appears to be sporadic, intermit, inconsistent. My desire is for you to create a life that is (for the most part) drama free, consistent, intentional, and so much more. It has been written, "Don't be afraid, little flock, for it is your Father's good pleasure to give you the kingdom." As we step away from the world (the temporary) and turn within (the eternal), we get to trust the essence of our Beingness—love, joy, peace, vitality, intelligence, abundance, etc.

10 Principles for A Life Worth Living—A Workbook for Actively and Purposefully Living Your Life is the third and last book in this series. We began with *10 Principles for A Life Worth Living—A Guide for Actively and Purposefully Living Your Life.*

Next came *10 Principles for A Life Worth Living—Practicing Spiritual Principles Daily Through the Use of Affirmations.* I have created these books as tools to remember to practice, practice, practice. With practice, we are destined to live a life where we have made an agreement with our greatness, our gloriousness, our Divine Nature.

10 Principles for A Life Worth Living—A Workbook for Actively and Purposefully Living Your Life is to be used in conjunction with my online courses, workshops, and individual or group Practitioner sessions. I have designed each of the *Ten Principles* to be facilitated as a thirty to sixty minute experience. You are meant to be guided and directed in a way that allows for your inward journey. You are meant to record/journal what is showing up in a particular moment to gain insights and assist in your transformation. There will be times when you will feel "stuck" and will need the assistance of listening, reflecting, and participating in a group dialogue or being asked questions through a Practitioner session. The pathway to transformation is practice. This workbook systematically creates that pathway. Please go to my website (www.KarenMillsAlston.com) or Instagram (@KarenMillsAlston) to calendar a Practitioner session or for information to attend my next workshop.

Here's to the fully activated, unique you! Begin practicing right now!

Blessings and love,

Karen Mills-Alston, ALSP

Acknowledgements

I am so grateful for my master teacher Michael Bernard Beckwith. Most of what I have remembered and realized as a Spiritual Being is through his teachings. I have studied with him for 17 years. I know the importance of having a consistent, loving, powerful practice because of his example. His lyrics to the song Trust Love are these: "Love is the essence of the Spirit that is know for always giving...." Thank you Rev. Michael for your YES! Thank you for letting me see what it looks like to trust, listen, obey, give, and love.

PRINCIPLE ONE

Begin Each Day in a Spirit of Gratitude

Gratitude is the sincerest prayer of the heart, arising from a recognition of the precious human incarnation each of us has been given. We then walk through life in humble awe of the realization that Spirit inseparably, purposely individualized itself as "me."

Michael Bernard Beckwith

****

Without judgment or comparison, think about how you woke up this morning. Describe what it felt like and what was on your mind as you awoke.

What is your practice of "getting up and moving" once you place your feet on the floor? What comes next?

Are you willing to shift into a Higher way of being, to begin your day creating that which you really want to experience? Explain your YES.

The Practice: How to *Begin Your Day With Gratitude*

Each morning, even before opening your eyes and thinking your first thought, begin the practice of saying to yourself, "I am so thankful for this new day and....", then identify a few things for which you are grateful. For example, some of the things I say to myself include: "As I awake I give thanks for another opportunity to express life—my beating heart, the joy of moving into my day feeling and expressing what is within me." Each morning the list varies, but what remains the same is the overall sense of gratitude arising from my heart.

What are you grateful for today?

As a "tone setter" what feeling tone are you consciously choosing to establish for your day?

Expanded Practices of *Begin with Gratitude*

- Deepen your practice of being grateful. As you rise in the morning, stay in this "attitude of gratitude" for at least 10 minutes. What you are no longer doing is creating a "to do" list. You ARE (in these few moments) establishing the tone for the remainder of your day. Move into meditation; play beautiful music; keep your thoughts HIGH. Whatever you do in these 10 minutes, STAY in this elevated place of gratitude. This practice simply begets more things for which to be grateful.

- Perhaps today, you woke up stuck, mad, upset at someone or something and you don't FEEL like being grateful. Take a breath. FEEL the stuckness, the anger, even the feeling of not wanting to be grateful. NOW become mindful of what Divine quality may "appear to be missing" in this particular moment—love, joy, abundance, peace, vitality, creativity, etc. FEEL that quality and radiate it throughout your body temple. Take another conscious breath. NOW remember that you have the strength to SHINE especially when you don't want to. This is your natural state of being. YOU are a body of power, strength, light, and Infinite possibilities. NOW you can CHOOSE to be grateful.

- As you are moving though your day, be grateful just for the opportunity to be grateful. Put a smile on your face, let your light shine. As an extension of your morning "wake up" practice, at 12 noon, 3 pm, and 6 pm, stop, take a breath and become grateful. Celebrate your life even before you have something to celebrate. Don't wait! Give thanks NOW.

- There are times in your life when you may feel that there are people, places, things, "forces" against you. Bring those individuals to mind individually or collectively. Thank them for showing up. Be grateful. They represent gifts in your life that (with practice) can allow you to become stronger, purposeful, powerful. Say to yourself: "I am more than this." "Everything is working together for my good." "I no longer give my power away. I stand in excellence." And then begin to feel the healing/revealing power of unconditional love. Love them right where they are. Be grateful for THAT!!

As you have chosen one or all of the Extended Practices of *Begin with Gratitude,* journal here about how it feels to move deeper and further in this practice. What did you notice about your willingness or your unwillingness to do so?

____

____

____

____

____

____

____

____

Insights and Transformation with the practice of *Begin with Gratitude*

Are you able to carry the feeling tone of gratitude throughout your day?

What is your intention as you continue to practice *Begin with Gratitude*? What does the new you look and feel like?

Affirmations

- **I am grateful for this new day and the opportunity to begin again.**
- **I am grateful for my strength to be the Real me.**
- **I am grateful that I have everything I need to fully express my Divine purpose.**

What more can you realize, affirm, and declare about yourself?

PRINCIPLE TWO

How to Listen from the Very Depths of Your Soul

If we are faithful in the practice of contemplation and the simpler form of meditation, this practice will lead us from one form of meditation to another, until we arrive at the actual experience of hearing the still small voice of reviving divine guidance from within, and being divinely led every step of the way.

Joel S. Goldsmith

****

What are you listening to? Is listening happening more from outside of yourself or more from within?

Where does the previous question resonate in your body temple? Detail any feelings that arise.

Do you currently have a meditation practice? Where, when, and how often do you meditate? If you have not established a practice begin to create it here.

The Practice: How to *Listen from the Very Depths of Your Soul*

Intentionally set aside time to daily sit, relax the body temple, still the mind, and consciously watch the breath, beginning with just 3 minutes. When distracting thoughts arise, view them as clouds passing in the sky and simply return to paying attention to your breath. Let your attention drop into your heart as you commune, attune, and listen for the intuitive voice of your Higher Self.

Are you available and willing to meditate for 3 minutes before you step out the door for your day? What does your willingness feel like? If you don't know, describe those feelings.

Is there anything that you need to release, let go of to allow a consistent meditation practice?

Expanded Practices of *Listening*

Broaden your meditation practice. After creating a period of morning meditation, stop spontaneously during your day and meditate for 3 minutes. There's always a place to meditate even if it's in the stall of a bathroom. This practice serves for the recalibration of your energy and a reminder that you are supported by a Presence that is more than any human experience. It's the true meaning of communing with the Presence moment to moment.

Practice sitting in meditation for 3 minutes each day for 3 weeks. Begin to establish a specific time in your day to do so. The next week add 2 minutes to your practice and meditate for 5 minutes; the following week, meditate for ten minutes; the following week, 15 minutes. Live stream or show up in person to Agape's Sunday 6:45 am Way of Meditation service. "Simply begin" as Michael Bernard Beckwith suggests.

There may be times in your morning when you become caught up in "time" and think there is not an opportunity to meditate. As you find yourself placing your hand on the front door of your home to leave for the day ask yourself "Have I meditated?" If the answer is "no" STOP, sit, relax the body temple, still the mind, and consciously watch the breath (meditate) for just 3 minutes. If you forget to ask that question, when you **DO** remember be loving and kind with yourself and begin again.

Begin to listen, not with your outer ear, with the ear behind the ear. This is the Presence, your intuition, your gut, your heart space speaking to you. Whatever you call it, listen to this powerful "still small voice" and obey it. It loves and adores you and is cheering you on for the Highest and best to unfold AS YOU! This may feel uncomfortable. Trust, surrender, and see what happens. It's beyond anything you may ever imagine with your human mind.

As you have chosen one or all of the Extended Practices of *Listening*, journal here about how it feels to move deeper and further in this practice. What did you notice about your willingness or unwillingness to do so?

As meditation is one of the seven Agape Spiritual Practices choose one other practice to be included in your daily practice…affirmative prayer, meditation, Life Visioning, sacred service, spiritual fellowship, spiritual study, and tithing. What practice did you choose and why? Are you practicing it?

Insights and Transformation with the practice of *Listening*

As you continue to meditate day to day, describe what changes occur in your life. For example, are you more intuitive? Are you more open to listen from your heart?

How are you feeling about meditation in this moment?

What is your intention as you continue to practice *Listening*? What does your meditation practice look and feel like now?

Affirmations

- **I listen and obey Spirit.**
- **I let go of any mind chatter and begin to listen with my heart.**
- **I trust Spirit as I am guided and directed moment to moment.**
- **I surrender, yield, and trust my Higher Self.**

What more can you realize, affirm, and declare about yourself?

PRINCIPLE THREE

Align with the Creative Power of Your Word

The human mind is like a fertile ground where seeds are continually being planted. The seeds are opinions, ideas and concepts. You plant a seed, a thought grows. The word is like a seed and the human mind is so fertile. What is important is to see which kind of seeds our mind is fertile for, and to prepare it to receive the seeds of love.

Don Miguel Ruiz

****

Describe yourself. What comes to mind FIRST when asked to do so?

What words or phrases do you use as you talk about yourself or others that do not affirm your True Nature?

What emotions arise with your realization that you have been telling lies about yourself and others…planting false seeds?

What is your new agreement with your Higher Self? What is your new conversation about yourself and others?

The Practice: How to *Align with the Creative Power of Your Word*

Begin to become aware of every word you speak and every thought you think about yourself. Perhaps you use words such as: stupid; dumb; unloveable; unworthy; not good enough. Make a list of these words. Each time you hear yourself using any of these words, take a breath and **replace** that word with words that describe your True Nature— I am brilliant; I am intelligent; I am lovable; I am worthy; I am good, grand, and glorious. This practice takes mindfulness and a willingness to remember who you Truly are.

Each morning and throughout the day claim your new identity. Wrap your arms around yourself, take a breath, and affirm out loud—"I am glorious! I am actively and purposefully living my life full out! Everything is working together for my good! All of my needs are met! I am available for abundance to be generously expressed through me! I am grateful to be the harmonious expression of love, joy, and peace NOW!" Feel the vibration of these words throughout your entire body. Repeat. Create your own unique affirmation. Say it out loud!

What have you noticed about yourself as you become aware of your new conversation about yourself and others?

What has challenged you the most with this new way of speaking about yourself and others?

Are you remembering to practice Principles One and Two when you may feel stuck? Explain your YES or NO.

Expanded Practices of *Aligning with the Creative Power of Your Word*

The mystic Ernest Holmes writes—"I affirm for others that which I accept for myself." This is a powerful way of realizing that that which we want for ourselves, we get to choose to want for others. Begin to become aware of every word you speak and every thought you think about others. Perhaps you describe some people as: lazy; an idiot; unreliable; not worth it; untrustworthy; fickle. Make a list of these words; take a breath and think about that person from your heart space. Begin describing that person with words that tell of their True Nature— she/he is kind, loving, compassionate, available, intelligent, wonderful. We call this Spiritually gossiping. You can start a new conversation about yourself AND others, it simply takes practice.

What are you listening to? Begin paying attention to the words in the music you are listening to. Are you empowered or uplifted? Pay attention to games, programs, social media you are involved with. Are you inspired or left feeling distressed and angry? If you need to, turn off the music, internet, TV. Listen to the still small voice. When you have practiced listening to people, places, and things that are a vibrational match with your Soul, you become a conscious, beneficial Presence for yourself and this planet.

Add the practice of Witness Consciousness to your Spiritual Practice. Witness (notice) yourself when a problem or an old pattern comes up. Witness your behavior; an emotion somewhere in your body. What is your mind saying to you? Feel the emotions that arise. Remind yourself that "I am more than this." Use affirmations to declare who you Really are. Make Witness Consciousness a lifetime practice.

As you have chosen one or all of the Extended Practices of *Aligning with the Creative Power of Your Word*, journal here about how it feels to move deeper and further in this practice. What did you notice about your willingness or unwillingness to do so?

___

___

___

___

___

___

___

___

___

___

___

Insights and Transformation with the practice of *Aligning with the Creative Power of Your Word*

As you continue to pay attention to your word, describe what changes occur in your life.

How are you feeling about the power of your word in this moment?

What is your intention as you continue to practice *Aligning with the Creative Power of Your Word?*

Affirmations

- **I am glorious!**
- **I am loved, adored, and appreciated ALWAYS!**
- **I am needed and significant.**
- **I am willing to be great, excellent, and magnificent.**
- **I am willing to allow the best version of myself emerge.**

What more can you realize, affirm, and declare about yourself?

PRINCIPLE FOUR

Be the First to Forgive

Keeping our hearts and minds free of the debris of resentment and animosity is achieved through the power of forgiveness and is vital to our spiritual awakening. The mark of spiritually mature individuals is that they are the first to forgive.

Michael Bernard Beckwith

Whether it is an offense against you, against democracy, against justice, against nations, or against the word of God, set them free. Release them. Ask God's forgiveness. Be willing that they be forgiven without penalty.

Joel S. Goldsmith

****

Make a list of people, place, things, institutions that trigger you, those things that stop you from moving forward.

What painful stories are you still holding onto about yourself and/or others?

Feel the emotions that emerge as you think about ways you have felt unheard, unseen, unsafe. Describe those emotions.

As you begin the forgiveness process, begin with yourself. Use this phrase "I forgive myself for..........." Make a list of things that you are willing to shift and transmute as you begin to forgive yourself.

The Practice: How to *Be the First to Forgive*

- All forgiveness begins with self-forgiveness. We are forgiving ourselves for feelings, emotions, and actions that have closed us off from our True Nature of loving kindness. This is a time to be especially gentle with yourself. Take a breath. Begin with a simple affirmation—"I forgive me." Let this affirmation fill your Soul. Sit with it, breathing through it, feeling that which comes up—sorrow, pain, anger, fear, etc. Listen to the words in this powerful song written by Tim McAfee-Lewis and performed by Charles Holt **https://www.youtube.com/watch?v=p_yqm_b4NxM.** Hear the words again…"I *forgive me. Everything that I've been holding on to, I let go. I surrender, I surrender. I'm ready for my change."* Repeat and repeat and repeat. Wrap your arms around yourself and say "I love you."

What have you noticed about yourself during this forgiveness activity?

What is the most difficult aspect for you about forgiveness?

Is there anything you find easy about forgiveness?

Expanded Practices of *Be the First to Forgive*

- Make a list of people you feel have hurt you. Be loving and kind with yourself. Begin with a simple affirmation—"I forgive you." Take a breath. Let this affirmation fill your Soul. Sit with it, breathing through it, feeling that which comes up—hurt, unworthiness, any should have, would have, could haves, etc. Read the names on your list out loud as you listen to the words in this powerful song written by Tim McAfee-Lewis and performed by Charles Holt **https://www.youtube.com/watch?v=p_yqm_b4NxM.** Hear the words again…"*I forgive me. Everything that I've been holding on to, I let go. I surrender, I surrender. I'm ready for my change.*" Repeat and repeat and repeat. Affirm—"I forgive you for having hurt me and know that there is peace between our Souls." It is not necessary for forgiveness to take place in person or in a conversation with someone. It must, however be a Spiritual Practice for transformation to occur.

- Make a list of people you believe you have hurt. Be gentle and loving with yourself. Take a breath and with each name say out loud—"Please forgive me." Feel the opening of your heart. You may also add—"Any way in which I have hurt you, please forgive me. I extend my heart's apology and bless and love you." Repeat and repeat and repeat. Forgiving yourself and others may take several sincere attempts, so appreciate yourself for your willingness to continue the process whether it takes hours, days, or even years.

- Forgiveness is an ongoing process; therefore, drop expectations and projections that forgiveness should happen the first time you apply these practices. As you are moving through your day a name or face may pop into your awareness. Practice affirming—"I forgive and I am forgiven." This is a powerful way to remember that you can speak your word at any moment, practice forgiveness, and be forgiven.

- As you continue to practice forgives, include it in your Spiritual Practice as you rise in the morning and as you go to sleep at night. Scan your sleep time. Was anything revealed in a dream as a reminder to forgive? Before sleep, scan your day. Is there anything that needs to be forgiven? No matter how small, forgive. Begin to practice forgiveness moment to moment. Forgive and then become open to love conditionally.

As you have chosen one or all of the Extended Practices of *Be the First to Forgive*, journal here about how it feels to move deeper and further in this practice. What did you notice about your willingness or unwillingness to do so?

____

____

____

____

____

____

____

____

____

Insights and Transformation with the practice of *Be the First to Forgive*

Is self forgiveness and the forgiveness of others becoming an ongoing process for you? Is there anything you continue to hold on to because you are unwilling to forgive?

How effective is forgiveness as a moment to moment activity in your life?

What is your intention as you practice *Be the First to Forgive?*

Affirmations

- **I forgive myself.**
- **I forgive and I am forgiven.**
- **I forgive. They know not what they do.**
- **I choose to love again, unconditionally.**

What more can you realize, affirm, and declare about yourself?

PRINCIPLE FIVE

How to Be Flexible and Open to Change

Get up, go to work, come home, go to bed. Get up, go to work, come home, go to bed. 5 days a week. Get up, go to work, come home, go to bed.

John W. Alston

****

Describe areas in your life needing change and thus far you have been unsuccessful to make a change or even become more flexible?

What painful stories are you still holding onto about yourself and/or others that stop you from living your life full out?

Feel the emotions that emerge as you think about ways you have felt unheard, unseen, unsafe. Describe those emotions.

If you were open and flexible, what would that best case scenario look like, feel like?

The Practice: How to *Be Flexible and Open to Change*

Opening ourselves to change is an intimate, vulnerable process. It is, in fact, one that requires authentic humility, a prerequisite for opening our hearts to flexibility, teachability, for entering the energy field of change. Doing so can be compared to the metaphor of the proverbial hero's journey wherein we begin an inner adventure of transformation, all the while knowing it is unpredictable, beyond our control, that challenges await us, yet every step is sacred, trustworthy, utterly worthwhile. We cross this threshold into change not by eliminating fear, but by being fearless about the fears that will inevitably arise. And like the hero, we struggle with the ego's resistance, reluctance, and apply skillful means in working with these challenges. When this journey has concluded—the timing of which is equally unpredictable—we return home to ourselves having been graced by a profound revolution and evolution in consciousness. This is the spiritual practitioner's unconditionally loving journey into "Yes," induced, guided, and blessed by the Spirit within.

Tools for Your Hero's Journey

Prepare by creating a list of habits, patterns, and false beliefs about yourself you desire to release. For example, I am not good enough; no one loves me; I get sick every Spring. Perhaps there are habits that have been in your family for generations. Really dig deeply no matter the pain or even embarrassment. List them here.

Take each habit, pattern, and false belief, one at a time. Close your eyes, take a deep breath and feel this LIE, let go of the so called power you think it has over you. Take another breath. Describe what it feels like if you choose to release this LIE. Be kind and compassionate with yourself. Offer tenderness towards the places in yourself you don't like or that scare you, inviting them to work with you on your journey.

Next, create a list of Divine qualities you want to remember as your True Essence—love, peace, beauty, etc.

Set aside time to contemplate these qualities. Do some practical research to identify their deepest aspects, how they express in everyday life. Are there individuals in your life or those you have experienced that radiate a particular quality? Use affirmations.

Extended Practice of how to *Be Flexible and Open to Change*

The Hero's Journey can be practiced time and time again. You have the technology. The Extended Practice is to use it!

As you have chosen to *Be Flexible and Open to Change*, journal here about how it feels to move deeper and further in this practice. What did you notice about your willingness or unwillingness to do so?

Insights and Transformation with the practice of *Being Flexible and Open to Change*

How have you changed with this practice? Are you now aware of speaking the Truth about who you are and no longer malpracticing?

What is your intention as you practice *Being Flexible and Open to Change*?

Affirmations

- **I honor the spiritual hero within me and invite it to come forth confidently, humbly, receptively.**
- **I release the need to control my journey and invite Spirit's grace to guide my footsteps all along the way.**
- **With every beat of my heart I open myself to change. I am flexible, receptive, teachable, and worthy of fulfilling my intentions.**
- **I now fearlessly work with fear by not pushing it away and by receiving the messages it is present to convey.**
- **I allow my Higher Self to introduce me to parts of myself I have yet to meet, and greet them with openness and love.**

What more can you realize, affirm, and declare about yourself?

PRINCIPLE SIX

Speak Kindly, Respectfully, Honestly, and Openly

The antidote for all friction is a realization of Oneness.

Joel S. Goldsmith

Our words are a creative force for transmitting kindness, compassion, and the wisdom of our hearts, which energetically vibrate within their recipients long after they are spoken.

Michael Bernard Beckwith

****

Take a moment and think about how you show up as you move through your day. How do you speak to others, for example, your work colleagues; the mail carrier; a server; a phone solicitor; a member of your family; your good friend.

Who are you "modeling." Describe the felling tone, in other words the "wake" or the Divine essence of this person (s).

What qualities describe your "wake."

Is there an opportunity to up level your "wake?"

The Practice: How to *Speak Kindly, Respectfully, Honestly, and Openly*

Every hour on the hour, stop close your eyes and sense how your body is feeling. If you are in a joyful place, give thanks. If you are feeling hurt, fearful, sad, feel those feelings. Vent when you can, alone. THEN, breath in and out gratitude, remembering all that there is to be grateful for. Put a smile on your face allowing joy to bubble up. This takes practice and it's your natural way of being. As you move through your day, continue to be aware of your feelings. It prepares you to live in the world and not of it, so when stuff happens, you are no longer the person who advances anger. You are available to BE peace. You are available to be kind.

As you have practiced this practice, what has worked really well?

Because you are either fine tuning who you are or transforming completely your way of being, describe any resistance to this practice.

What are you choosing to let go?

What Divine qualities have emerged with this practice?

Extended Practice of how to *Speak Kindly, Respectfully, Honestly, and Openly*

Speaking, communicating is what you do moment to moment. How do you become an effective, powerful, loving communicator not only with yourself, with immediate family, close friends, and work colleagues? This may unfold with specific agreements, that create a consistent feeling of harmony, safety and support for discussions and arguments. Whether or not another individual in your life wishes to enter into these agreements with you, remember that you practice these agreements first and foremost *for yourself*, for your own evolving practice of communicating with your heart.

Agreement One: Disagree or argue in the "now," without rehashing facts and feelings from the past. The "past" means yesterday, last week, last month which prevents sidetracking from the main point, reopening old wounds, and wasting time.

Agreement Two: Speak in the first person of "I," instead of "You," which glaringly points the finger of blame at the other person. "You" is a surefire way to escalate an argument and prevent resolution, whereas "I" takes responsibility for one's own feelings, allowing them to openly and honestly express, giving the other individual the opportunity to better let them in. For example, "I have the impression that…." or, "It's my feeling that…"

Agreement Three: No name-calling or assigning of labels, for no argument is resolved by calling a person a name other than their own. Doing so completely crosses the line of respect and love and can devastate a relationship. Even when addressing a person by their name, the tone in which it is done is equally contributory to being respectful. As well, "labels" also should not be assigned to another individual, as in "Well, you're just being 'Mr.—or Ms.—Know-It-All!'"

Argument Four: Stay in the room. Even if you have to call a time out, if possible remain in the room. Storming out creates drama, exacerbates the anger, and simply isn't productive. If, however, you must step away in order to cool down, before you leave the room agree upon a designated time to continue your conversation.

Agreement Five: Hug it out, shake hands, or agree to disagree, whatever is required for both parties to understand that the argument has satisfactorily concluded.

Which agreement impacted you the most? How?

____

____

____

____

____

____

____

____

As you have chosen one or all of the Extended Practice of how to *Speak Kindly, Respectfully, Honestly, and Openly* journal here about how it feels to move deeper and further in this practice. What did you notice about your willingness or unwillingness to do so?

Insights and Transformation with the practice of how to *Speak Kindly, Respectfully, Honestly, and Openly*

How have you integrated this practice into your life? How has your life been transformed because of it?

What is your intention as you practice to *Speak Kindly, Respectfully, Honestly, and Openly*?

Affirmations

- **I am fully aware of my thoughts, words, and actions as I speak to myself and with others.**
- **My wake is loving, kind, generous, and joyful.**
- **I am here for my good and the good of all.**
- **I am no longer reacting with anger, hurt or fear, I am responding knowing that Spirit is in the midst of it all.**

What more can you realize, affirm, and declare about yourself?

PRINCIPLE SEVEN

Live in the Yes Zone

"Yes" is about living in a co-creative partnership with Spirit, with infinite possibilities. Embedded in our soulware, the Yes Factor is just waiting to be discovered and activated.

Michael Bernard Beckwith

****

Become aware of where you land in the YES or NO Zone. What is your general, typical response when your availability is questioned?

Do you sometimes feel obligated to say YES, when you really want to say NO? How/where did you learn that?

Is there a pattern of not honoring yourself with a NO?

The Practice: How to *Live In the YES Zone*

"Yes I am available! Yes I am willing! Yes I can!" More than words, such statements are a state of consciousness. Our YES makes space for our dreams to manifest, for our lives to to be fully expanded and lived without hesitation. Begin paying attention when you say YES! What does it feel like? Do you feel like the powerful Being that you are? Or is there something else that comes up—unworthiness, not good enough? Do you expand or contract with your YES! Listen. Pay attention to your personal pattern of saying Yes! Journal about it.

The Extended Practice: How to *Live In the YES Zone*

Begin to pay attention when you say NO. What's the feeling tone in your NO? Is it said from a place of anger? Is it said from a place of a past experience of hurt or anger? Are there specific circumstances when you use NO?

For a Life Worth Living

When we say NO to negativity, something has to occupy its former space because we don't live, move, and have our being in a void. So why not consider letting YES become a permanent resident? Now this isn't about denial, bypass, or sticking your head in the sand, because we must be honest about feelings of disappointment, hurt, and so on. Setting a fertile ground opens the mind and heart to limitless possibilities. I invite you to begin observing and journaling those areas in your life to which you have said YES and the results that followed.

Begin observing and journaling those areas in your life to which you have said NO and the results that followed. In this way you can note when a YES served you well, when a NO opened the space for a YES, and begin establishing a new pattern for the proactive, impactful use of these powerful words.

As you have chosen one or all of the Extended Practices of how to *Live in the YES Zone* journal here about how it feels to move deeper and further in this practice. What did you notice about your willingness or unwillingness to do so?

Insights and Transformation with the practice of how to *Live in the YES Zone*

How have you integrated this practice into your life? How has your life been transformed because of it?

What is your intention as you continue to practice to *Live in the YES Zone*? What does the new you look and feel like?

Affirmations

- **Yes I am available! Yes I am willing! Yes I can!**
- **I am available to experience more good than I can possibly imagine.**
- **I am the fullness of a friendly Universe that is in support of my potentiality.**
- **I am strong, renewed, and I welcome the newness of my live!**

What more can you realize, affirm, and declare about yourself?

PRINCIPLE EIGHT

Appreciate—And Say it Out Loud

In all things give thanks.

Michael Bernard Beckwith

Gratitude is not related to an expectancy of what we may receive tomorrow. Gratitude is the sharing or expressing of joy for the good already received.

Joel S. Goldsmith

****

Think about how you give. Is it with an agenda, with the expectation of being acknowledged and appreciated?

At any time, does it seem that your feelings go unseen/unheard?

Is there a willingness to give without expecting anything in return? What emotions emerge as this question is asked?

The Practice: How to *Awaken an Appreciative Heart*

Today, begin with appreciating yourself! Observe things that you like about yourself. Write them down. Read the list to yourself. Go ahead, talk to yourself out loud, write yourself a thank you letter, sing out your self-appreciation. Because you deserve it! Love and appreciate your willingness to do what you do--how you show up in your neighborhood, your family, your office. Don't wait for someone to tell you. Tell yourself, as often as you desire: "I appreciate ME." Notice if this practice makes a difference in your life. Notice that you may be feeling happier, carefree, and even joyful. Journal here about this practice.

The Extended Practice: How to *Awaken an Appreciative Heart*

After a week of the proceeding practice, continue appreciating YOU and now include others in your appreciating, telling them out loud from family, friends, neighbors, Lyft drivers, sales clerks, waitresses, to parking attendants—all those you encounter throughout any given day. Let the mail carrier know how much you appreciate the delivery of mail 6 days a week; give the parking attendant a smile with a compliment and a word of appreciation; tell a coworker how happy it is to work with him or her; give a kiss or a hug to someone and tell him or her how special they are to you. Let your day be filled with words of appreciation for yourself and others. There is no such thing as doing too much of this practice.

For a Life Worth Living

Write down what you are currently grateful for in your life—loved ones, friends, pets, your home, car, gardener, housekeeper, doctor, dentist, Spiritual Practitioner—is your consciousness-expanding, heart-opening?

As you have chosen one or all of the Extended Practices of how to *Awaken an Appreciative Heart,* how it feels to move deeper and further in this practice. What did you notice about your willingness or unwillingness to do so?

Insights and Transformation with the practice of how to *Awaken an Appreciative Heart*

How have you integrated this practice into your life? How has your life been transformed because of it?

What is your intention as you continue to practice to *Awaken an Appreciative Heart*
What does the new you look and feel like?

Affirmations

- **I appreciate myself each and every moment in deep, deep gratitude.**
- **Life is good. I am grateful.**
- **I create joy, peace, and harmony with each word and every thought.**
- **I withhold nothing. I live AS the fullness of the Presence.**

What more can you realize, affirm, and declare about yourself?

PRINCIPLE NINE

Be Generous in Giving and Being of Service

Let your life be a life of givingness. Give out of the infinity, which you are. Give out of the infinite boundless supply.
Joel S. Goldsmith

Through all forms of giving we become a channel through which the Spirit gives of itself. The question of a generous heart is, "Where and how can I be of service?" As we spiritually evolve, we give to live until we live to give.
Michael Bernard Beckwith

****

Take a moment and bring to mind a person in your life or on this planet who is generous and giving. Describe that person using Divine attributes.

What feelings arise within you as you think about this person? Is there any comparison happening?

If money was not an issue and you could create, give, BE, anything you desired for yourself, your friends and family or the planet, what would that look like?

What's stopping you from fulfilling this desire?

The Practice: How to *Be Generous in Giving and Being of Service*

***As we spiritually evolve, we give to live until we live to give.* Michael Bernard Beckwith.**

Volunteering, giving, serving, whatever you call it is always a way to participate in the Law of Circulation—giving and receiving. Most desire to have something tangible in hand FIRST before giving. As Infinite beings, we get to give from a place of our willingness to remember that we already have everything we need. As you begin each day, become mindful of opportunities to give. Here is an example: give thanks— at meals; for the new day; for the movement of your body temple; for your friends and family. This requires nothing more than your availability to choose. How do you give without even thinking about it?

The Extended Practice: How to *Be Generous in Giving and Being of Service*

As you move through your day, continue giving thanks. Now add to this givingness an act of service. Notice police cars, fire trucks, ambulances that are moving through your neighbor whether driving or with sirens blaring. Take a breath and evoke a prayer of thanksgiving for their service; their safety; the dynamic well being of those they are serving. Remember that harmonizing good is happening as they arrive to their destination for themselves and those they are responding to. This is such a powerful way of being a beneficial Presence on the planet. Make this practice a consistent way of service and giving.

Choose now to serve in a Higher, deeper, wider way. Pray to be guided and directed to serve within an organization that will contribute to mutually nurturing you and its cause. Trust and follow through on your inner guidance. Agape International Spiritual Center may be a perfect place for you to begin to serve. The benefit of serving is to be in community with like minded individuals; to meet new friends; to give in ways that can not be measured; to open your heart; so much more. Choose now to serve.

As you have chosen one or all of the Extended Practices of how to *Be Generous in Giving and Being of Service,* how does it feel to move deeper and further in this practice. What did you notice about your willingness or unwillingness to do so?

Insights and Transformation with the practice of how to *Be Generous in Giving and Being of Service*

How have you integrated this practice into your life? How has your life been transformed because of it?

What is your intention as you continue to practice to *Be Generous in Giving and Being of Service?* What does the new you look and feel like?

Affirmations

- **I am a generous Being.**
- **I give unconditionally, straight from my heart.**
- **I remember that as I give, everyone is lifted up, especially me!**

What more can you realize, affirm, and declare about yourself?

PRINCIPLE TEN

Be in Joy NOW!

Anywhere at any time you can practice what I call a "Face Asana"—the face pose—no yoga mat required! All you have to do in the midst of any mindset or circumstance is remind yourself of the unconditional joy of Spirit that infuses your being. Then watch how a radiant smile spreads across your face, blessing you and all those who cross your path.

Michael Bernard Beckwith

****

Close your eyes, take a breath become heart centered and begin to think about what brings you joy. List those things here.

How often do you incorporate these things in your life?

Do you feel worthy to *Be in Joy* moment to moment? Detail your response.

The Practice: How to *Be in Joy Now*

Sometimes your JOY is the source of your smile, but sometimes your smile can be the source of your JOY. Thich Nhat Hanh. JOY is the nature of Spirit and therefore it is our nature. One of the ways we remember this way of being is by smiling. This is a powerful practice because we know that joy is fueling us AND when we smile, we give thanks for a heart centered life! How does smiling more feel?

The Extended Practice: ***How to Be in Joy Now***

Laugh, smile, be in JOY now! As you move through your day become aware of what happens as you practice this. Here's a clue—it's contagious. JOY breaks out all around you with this practice.

Become still and contemplate what allows you to remember that JOY is within you always. Make a list of those things. NOW be inspired by participating in those things. Perhaps your list includes volunteering; making a phone call to someone; attending a concert; laughing out loud as you are watching your favorite comedian perform. Whatever it is—activate it by your participation.

As you have chosen one or all of the Extended Practices of how to *Be in Joy Now,* how does it feel to move deeper and further in this practice. What did you notice about your willingness or unwillingness to do so?

Insights and Transformation with the practice of how to *Be in Joy Now*

How have you integrated this practice into your life? How has your life been transformed because of it?

What is your intention as you continue to practice to *Be in Joy Now?* What does the new you look and feel like?

Affirmations

- **I am living AS joy now!**
- **My essence is the playful nature of joy.**
- **I am always allowing joy AS my life.**

What more can you realize, affirm, and declare about yourself?

Notes/Insights

Notes/Insights

Notes/Insights

Notes/Insights

Notes/Insights

Now What?

Begin again. Use this workbook over and over and over. Practice, practice, practice remembering that LIFE IS INFINITE. There is always an opportunity to go deeper, wider, and higher. When you think you're "there" you'll find out "there" is nonexistent. When our hearts are open, we discover so much more to be realized!

I would enjoy hearing from you. Feel free to contact me at www.karenmillsalston.com or direct message me on Instagram @KarenMillsAlston.

About the Author

A daughter and granddaughter of Practitioners in the New Thought-Ageless Wisdom tradition of spirituality, Karen Mills-Alston has literally been on her spiritual path since childhood. In her award-winning book series, ***10 Principles for a Life Worth Living*** she shares the rich legacy of three generations of women who have devoted their lives to spiritual principles and practices.

After graduating from the University of Southern California with a degree in political science, Karen became a lobbyist for the City of Los Angeles; later lobbied for the Air Transport Association; and was the Regional Government Vice President for Alaska Airlines and Southwest Airlines.

Today, Karen is an international speaker, offering transformational workshops, based on the teachings of Michael Bernard Beckwith. Karen serves as a volunteer on Agape's Board of Trustees; as the Interim Dean of Agape University; an instructor in Agape's Practitioner Student Studies; and Director of Agape's annual Revelation Conference. As an Agape Licensed Spiritual Practitioner (ALSP), she has a robust clientele that enthusiastically studies and practices the teachings found in ***10 Principles for a Life Worth Living***. Karen is the mother of Lindsay whom she says, "Everyday she reminds me how easy it is to love."

Made in the USA
Las Vegas, NV
08 March 2021

19179182R10081